God
Made Me

written by Linda L. Boyer
illustrated by Lorraine Arthur

Seventh Printing, 1993

Library of Congress Catalog Card Number 81-50677
©1981, The STANDARD PUBLISHING Company, Cincinnati, Ohio
Division of STANDEX INTERNATIONAL Corporation. Printed in U.S.A.

If God had made me a circle
instead of a little boy,
I'd be round like the silver moon
or roll like a bouncing toy.

If God had made me a triangle
instead of a girl with red hair,
I'd have a point like an ice cream cone
or stand tall like a tent at the fair.

If God had made me a square
instead of a child with curly locks,
I'd have four sides like my dollhouse
or hold toys like my toy box.

If God had made me an oval
instead of a freckle-faced lass,
I'd be like a stone from the sea
or sit like an egg on dune grass.

If God had made me a rectangle
instead of a child so bright,
I'd chime at noon like our
   grandfather clock
or fly high like my big box kite.

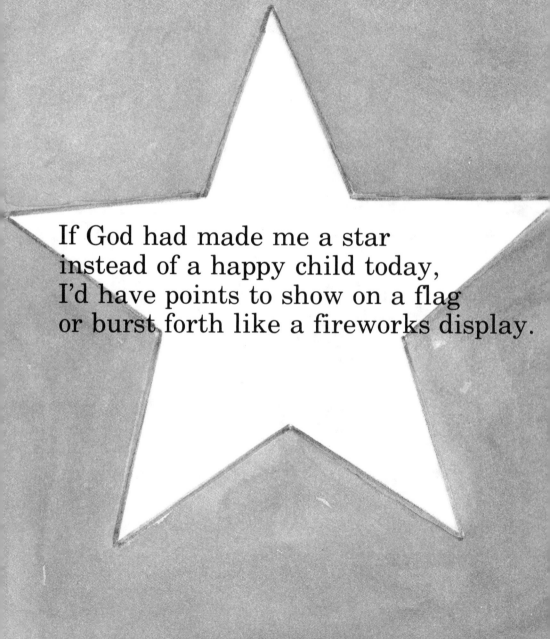

If God had made me a star
instead of a happy child today,
I'd have points to show on a flag
or burst forth like a fireworks display.

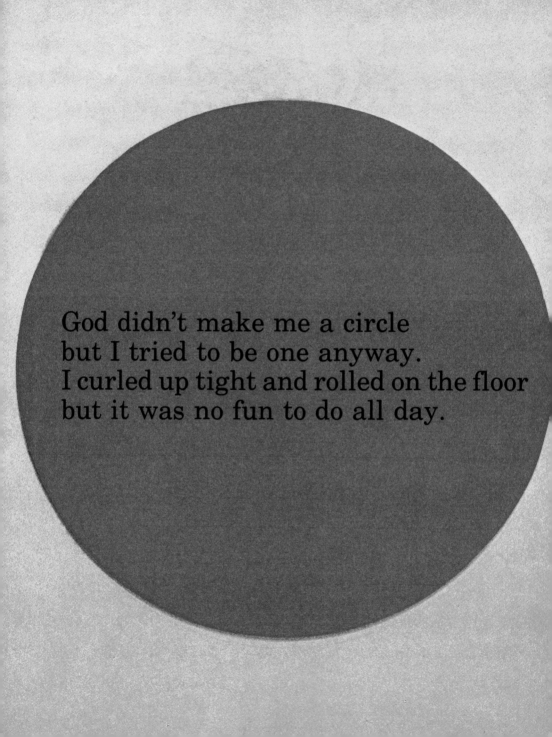

God didn't make me a circle
but I tried to be one anyway.
I curled up tight and rolled on the floor
but it was no fun to do all day.

Then I tried to be a square,
it sounded like great fun to me,
But my sides are not equal—
   I'm rounded a bit
and square I simply cannot be.

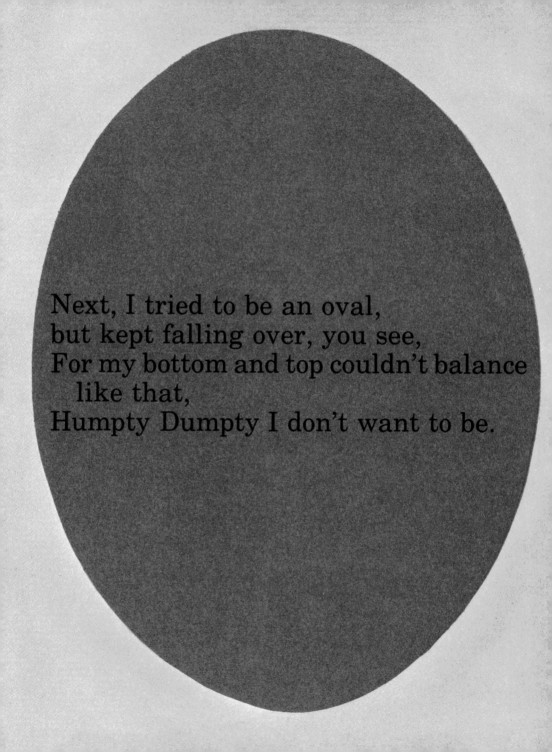

Next, I tried to be an oval,
but kept falling over, you see,
For my bottom and top couldn't balance
   like that,
Humpty Dumpty I don't want to be.

Finally I tried to be a star
but much to my dismay,
my feet and my arms tied in a knot.
I couldn't go outside and play.

I'm sure God knew what He was doing,
when He gave me two arms, two legs,
and eyes.
For my size, my shape, I'm just right!
God certainly is wise.

God didn't make me a triangle,
a circle, or even a square.
But I'm glad He made me just as I am.
"Thank You, dear God for Your care."